THE COMPANY MISERY LOVES

THE COMPANY MISERY LOVES

POEMS

KATE FOX

Sheila-Na-Gig Editions

ISBN: 9781962405058
Library of Congress Control Number: 2024939228

Sheila-Na-Gig Editions
Russell, KY
Hayley Mitchell Haugen, Editor
www.sheilanagigblog.com

Acknowledgments

Many thanks to the editors of the following journals and anthologies, in which these poems, some in earlier versions and with different titles, first appeared:

Crazy River: "The Courage to Travel," "Human Nature"
Cutthroat: "The Lost Child Poem"
Great River Review: "The Heaven of Lost Limbs"
Green Mountains Review: "Biblical Terms," "The Lazarus Method," "Summons"
Eight: 12th Annual Juried Reading: "Museum at the Tomb of the Unknowns"
Follow the Thread, Alan Cohen, ed.: "Mary Shelley: Heart of Hearts"
The Ides of March: An Anthology of Ohio Poets, Hannah Stephenson, ed.: "Making Love During a Terrorist Attack"
Kentucky Poetry Review: "Seibert, Colorado, 1963"
Mount Hope: "Kathleen Scott: Masks for Facial Disfigurement, WWI"
New Virginia Review: "The Illusion of Choice"
New Ohio Review: "A Summer Wind, a Cotton Dress," "Make No Mistake," "That Evening Sun"
Valparaiso Poetry Review: "No More," "Kathleen Scott Young's Tribute to George Mallory"
West Branch: "The Era of Reduced Expectations"
Windsor Review: "West Union Cemetery"

Some of these poems also appeared in *The Lazarus Method*, No. 12, in the Wick Chapbook Poetry Series I, published by the Kent State University Press, Kent, Ohio, and in *Walking Off the Map*, published by Seven Kitchens Press, Cincinnati, Ohio.

Dedicated to the four loves of my life:
Brandi Mitchell, Bob DeMott, Donna Spencer,
and June Berkley, who all contributed to this book.

Contents

I. Stories We Tell Ourselves

II. Stocking Up for the End of Days

I wouldn't interfere for the world, the world being //
everything this isn't, this unknown buried in the known.

—Irene McKinney, "Visiting My Gravesite:
Talbott Churchyard, West Virginia"

I. Stories We Tell Ourselves

The Illusion of Choice

And what would you like to be when you grow up?
Elsewhere.

Say you could have been raised
by wolves—mange-festered, feral,

starving for the last thrash of a rabbit,
the more calculated ambush of a deer.

Or say the opera had adopted you
at birth, the final aria of a dwindling

company gone bankrupt with passion,
your sable coat the only remnant

of their worth. But no, you chose
to be born here, among towns

like Flagler, Bovina, Seibert, Bethune,
places you pass through on your way

to somewhere else, unless you
live here—then you stay,

thinking the name on the water tower
means you, or that oil mixed with rain

in a hubcap is beautiful, which it is
because you own it, or think you do,

in your hand-me-down jacket
and the galoshes you wear

for cowboy boots, galloping along
past Hedgecoke's Grocery, Eunice's Cafe,

on your way to face some stranger.

Seibert, Colorado, 1963

Every summer an endless
row of combines paddled into fields,
swallowing waves of pale wheat.
The harvest crew, copper-shouldered,
dust-streaked, didn't bother
to bathe before they fell
between crisp sheets
stenciled "Seibert Hotel."

Across the street, we played
one-two-three-red-light
in a town so small we'd never seen one.
Our goal was the single corner streetlamp
haloed by a cloud of droning bugs.
As we flew past, yelling, "Home!"
some would fall and strike
at our feet.

Out of this light,
fieldhands would grapple
with our sisters.
They'd marry,
settle like pale dust
across Western Kansas.

I hear most of Northeastern
Colorado is irrigated now,
the harvest crews smaller,
fewer combines.
But one is enough.
Its Möbius blade engulfs
a game where if you're "it"
and look back,
everything freezes.

The Tick of a Pendulum

Roofers are back with their tar mops and buckets,
swabbing leaks that sound like gunfire

on the rim of roasters, the bottom of stockpots,
the floor a firing range of enamelware.

The ceiling bellies down toward the rug.
My mother takes up the slack, inhales formaldehyde,

swabs swollen boards with rags torn from bed sheets,
T-shirts, pillowcases, towels, sometimes even

a sundress, stripped of buttons, wash-faded, frayed.
"How many times do you have to be told?"

Her cadence matches the swing of the belt as I dance
at the end of her arm, my feet and new canvas shoes

tar-coated, palms stinging with each leather slap.
Later, she scrubs my feet pink with mineral spirits,

pulls me upright with a comb, rubber band so tight
my temples throb. "Maybe next time you'll know better,"

she says as she locks the pink rollers on the Maytag
with bleach-scalded hands, feeds two good outfits,

catalog-ordered for my brother and me, and my father's
gray twill shirts with his name above the pocket,

and her own thrift-store cotton dresses, thin
as dishtowels, pressing them flat as the Eucharist.

Now, years later, at the age she was then, I am still learning
how to know better—how warm tar must feel on bare feet,

how raindrops can depend indefinitely from one spot
in the ceiling while another spot pours like a sieve,

how divots of water against metal can lull
like the tick of a clock and still bring down a house.

And Their Forecast
—For Brandi

I can still hear my mother's defense:
"I did the best I could at the time."
Which was right, her worth defined

by which fork we used, or the greater necessity
of shining hair, clean skin, the "personal care"
pamphlets I threw away in favor of how

we might be with our bodies: naked, unashamed.

I relied on the past to teach you—the slant
of her arm across your chest, the cool press
of her palm to your forehead when the world

was dizzy with snow and you could barely breathe.
The whistle of the vaporizer was her wisdom, too,
its lukewarm air curled around us like licorice.

Unwittingly, she taught us well how to sicken and heal.

Now I unravel my days with her rituals and habits
as every day your face grows more beautiful, distant.
I have taught you proper manners and speech,

and once in humid summer, the Latin names
of clouds and their forecast. You can still remember
"Mammatus," pendulous black, boiling across Nebraska.

But what else? What else have I forgotten
in these daily rhythms we raise out of silence?
We all did our best, but what if it wasn't enough,

was never enough, for any of us?

Make No Mistake

You *are* the company misery loves.
Or at least does not neglect.
You take your pain seriously enough
to feel it like a missing leg, grieve for it
as your parents grieved for starving children
or birth defects—a curiously abstract loss—
but somehow relieved through
the March of Dimes or UNICEF.

Yet somehow loss took shape in those evenings
that trudged from house to house, collecting hope
from even the poorest of neighbors—took
the form of animals sturdy enough to follow
strangers into the street and come back,
their heads misshapen by the asphalt.
And later how they simply

disappeared, like the man who
said he would call and didn't,
and how you had him dead in Alabama,
Tennessee. How he, too, had simply
disappeared, and then, how you had wished
him dead, instead of merely fallible.

It isn't as if you could have loved
and chose not to.

It isn't that sort of choice at all.

Dinner at the Manifest Restaurant

I don't love you enough to tell you

that this vague sickness passing through
the table into the breaded veal and potatoes
is proximity
made unbearable by the distraction
of wine, convex and bleeding
over the lip of the goblet.

Nor do I love you enough

to tell you that I refuse to accept this
steady disintegration of a Sunday—
when the week has slid downhill
on all fours, and you wait for the light
to drop with some grace
behind the ridge, wait, backlit,
looking out on what has ultimately become
the cruelty of your life: this cul-de-sac
with its ledge of forced narcissus,
and before you, your hands
puckered by the slick and tepid water.

I want to tell you I don't love you

enough to admit the identity of this cuisine,
these thin-sleeved afternoons that can slip into frost
just as everyone has traded their coats for amazement,
and even the goldfinches are taken in enough to expect
fresh berries with the thaw. Yet here we sit, party
to the same old digressions: pleasure and sweat,
flesh that loves itself, regardless.

Getting Engaged in the Gun Room of the Lafayette Hotel

He snaps open the ring box and suddenly
it's high noon at this table, where black hats
and white, good guys and bad, all belly up

to the bar. Behind them, long rifles line the walls,
while Derringers, Schmidts, and Smith & Wessons
hang in shadowboxes shaped like tombstones.

I want to call him out. "This love ain't big enough
for the both of us!" hoping he'll turn tail, but his mind
is already on that long, long trail, that last cattle drive,

that moment when he will stare down the bore
of a very long Colt 45 and need a faithful sidekick
to step up and take one square in the chest.

No More

> "There's nothing written in the Bible… that says,
> 'If you believe in Me, you ain't going to have no troubles.'"
>
> —Ray Charles

A thin-wristed woman, I might have made the cut.
And you surely fit my M.O.: dark-skinned, brilliant,
difficult, and addicted, with a voice unearthed from some
ancient burial ground of grief, the suit, the sunglasses,

the escort, all conferring respect on such an unlikely
prospect. Clean-shaven, quiet, well-mannered, assured,
(though that last might have been the heroin), you were my
perfect bad boy. When told to hit the road, you just smiled,

offered excuses empty as pockets, made them sing it again,
then moaned "Aw, Baby," when you failed to win them over.
Nobody could whisper "Baby" like you, raw sex and affection,
romance, hunger, religion, all cooked down into those sad

old refrains: that grace can be had for a song,
that even bad love can save you.

Mary Shelley: Heart of Hearts

"I think on the heart in which the imagination
of [the deed] was conceived."
                                    —Mary Shelley

Trelawny raked it from your ribcage, tempered it
in waves that scoured the shore like a dishrag. Byron,
sickened by the body's watery ooze, staggered into the surf,

as Trelawny wrapped his blistered fist in gauze,
swaddled the rest around your stubborn heart, slipped it
into his pocket for the journey back to Pisa.

Ferrogosto: Assumption of the Blessed Virgin. Revelers
danced in the piazza, as skyrockets bloomed like spirea,
drizzled their fiery seed into the crowd, as beside me,

a woman, backlit, whispered, "And your husband, my dear?
Where might he be tonight?" I closed my eyes to the burning.
What bones could cradle it? What body could bear its weight?

I loved you, Shelley, or thought I did. To believe otherwise
would have damned me, too, and I had the living to consider.
So I wrapped the mineral fist in copies of "Adonais," kept it

long after you offered my body to Hogg as "common
treasure," even after you complained of my "conjugal neglect."
I, whose grief unleashed a monster, kept your work alive

after the bonfire consumed everything that would burn, leaving
only that defiant, calcified muscle in the ash. *And what of it now,*
you ask, *with all of us long dead?* I answer with fair copies of poems,

letters stripped of their "Hellenic strain," the curls of three infants
in small lockets, and the one flawed creature I loved beyond all reason
Because, even nameless, it hunched over its creator's body and wept.

Cleaning the House to Robert Earl Keen's *Happy Prisoner*

This world is not my home, but someone has to clean it,
has to live as if manner-born for these chores, hot corn,
cold corn, down in the kitchen, great God Almighty
nudging me, a pilgrim and a stranger, right down

the righteous path of servitude. I have acquired
such an aptitude for cleaning: the sharp scent of Pine-Sol,
dish towels bleached within a thread of heavenly white,
a holy host of coat hangers ready to take the weight

of this world upon their shoulders. But really, Mr. Keen,
isn't some form of service at the very heart of these ballads?
"The Long Black Veil" or "Poor Ellen Smith"? I wish I could
break the old watch and chain of faithfulness and betrayal,

wash down the walls of time where these tunes bleed through
like water stains. Instead, I sling the vacuum across the carpet,
singing high lonesome to "99 Years for One Dark Day,"
pretending these folk songs have nothing to do with me.

My Grandmother Attends
the Athens Quilt National, 1979

In her world, the fabric recovers what it once
clothed, garments stained or worn so thin
that she had to salvage the best with scissors,
then rock the treadle to piece corduroy to wool

to flannel in a starburst that, like a wood fire,
warms three times. Nothing frivolous, nothing
fancy, except for a burial quilt too bleak to abide
that she edged in lace and pearl buttons taken

from the baptismal dress. Under "Do Not Touch,"
she fingers a manatee's taffeta fins, the tessellated cape
of a matador, and finally, a school of Escher fish

that shifts into a skein of geese as the pattern moves
from sea to sky. She finally says, "You know, they
did their best, but these quilts aren't nothing but art."

Snowfall, Late Afternoon

I.

To look back over the dying and the dead
for some wisdom in suffering, long winters
at the feeder that seem like every gesture,
lingering phrases on the lips of a man who
is afraid, not of dying, but of the dying of others,
as she strokes his hair, as he sits at his desk,
watching the feeder swing with the weight of pursuit,
as he watches the keel and waver of a cardinal,
the bruised flutter in the air after hunger.

II.

She awakens next to the dream he tells her:
a streetcar and the friends who cannot tell him
the way home and how after he forgets about
going, he sees the street, the face in the window
like some bouquet belonging only to her,
and he returns to her for the keys. But her
dreams are all of dismemberment: men driven
by sin and revenge, blood and blunder,
desperate at the edge of the bed.

III.

She thumbs through these faces carefully,
recalling all the moves they ever made,
quilts around shoulders of an heirloom
mirror, the delicate wrestle of many
men to ease it flat to the mattress
where it reflects the sky over the pick-up
like a floor, angle of roof, regimen of leaves
that imply replication is at least worth considering.

To stand tall at such an angle, to find
some method of straddling it without falling,
perhaps this, then, would reveal the way the world
gives up its tender intent, much as flowers give off
the one color they can't absorb, as if deception
itself were the only landscape.

The National Geographic Society Awards
Josephine Peary a Medal, May 6, 1955

"[The] news arrived by ship that Peary had lost eight
toes to frostbite and had gained an Inuit mistress."
—Patricia Erikson

"Put it back in the box," I tell Marie, who accepted the medal
given to me 50 years too late. "I can't read it, anyway."
Yet I know the raised letters spell out "Mrs. Robert E. Peary"
as surely as the marriage license replaced my surname with his.
"How much do you think it would it be worth melted down?"
At 93, I can say these things because they expect me to be senile.
"Oh, Mother," Marie sighs and snaps the velvet box shut.

The ptarmigan were fat and easy to shoot, their breast meat
as succulent as a pintail's. I bagged and cleaned my share:
foxes, hares, an occasional seal, but on that day Astrup emptied
his Winchester into a herd of reindeer, missing them all. Except for one
that ran, then fell, then ran, then fell again. As we came over a rise,
we saw the fawn beside her. She rose again, and they made for the lake.
We followed. Our provisions were low. We needed the meat.

The fawn swam beside her, bolstering her up, but we knew
she couldn't last in the water. Finally she faltered, and we waded in,
pulled her to shore by velvet horns. Only then did the fawn break
for safety. The men had spent their ammunition, so it fell to me,
the one with the loaded pistol to end to the doe's suffering. I couldn't.
I stood up and handed the gun to Astrup, who took aim and fired
as the fawn bounded over the ice, disappeared into the rocks.

I think about that hunt even now. More than the birth of my daughter
above the Arctic Circle, swaddling her in sealskins as twilight fell.
More than the Eskimo girl I recognized from my husband's "ethnographic
photo" of her sitting naked—except for a shell necklace—among the rocks.
Even more than the gray-eyed baby boy she brought aboard the *Windward*
and introduced as my husband's. I see that reindeer and her fawn break
for the water, and just to feel what it's like to choose, I let them get away.

29

Rainsford J. Winslow Addresses a Patron of the Arts

"Broken our strength, yea, as crushed reeds we fall,
And yet the art, the art goes on."
—Ezra Pound, "The Decadence"

I've been unable to digest
my portion of tonight's dinner
carried out over the topic of Vivian Sissler
whose father played J. S. Bach and died.
She is still wearing black after thirty-five years
and eats at the Betsy Mills Club
for Classical Music,
and if "Jesu, Joy of Man's Desiring"
is thundering out over the humble voices
of Eternal Covenant Church,
she'll be there in the chancel
like a crow.

Or Marjorie DeWeese, her driveway streaks
the rust of welded scrap-iron—contours like a jawline
by DaVinci. She welds in a chiffon robe
the remnants of her kitchen: sardine tins,
old coffee cans, their strips spiraling down
like distorted members.
This is metalwork at its best—
a wresting of forms from their mortar,
these human branches reaching armless
for their maker. And tonight
we have them all

at the Betsy Mills Club.
Alistar Siltz with his invalid wife
and his paintings of textured bark,
Reese Planchett who proclaims his sister
to be Jane Eyre as the meat is being passed,
and me, my own hand-bound volumes

threaded here and there among the starch
of an after-dinner brandy. Bereaved,
I listen as Vivian hums "Cantata 29" beside me
like a reed being pulled
when it's wet.

Summons

"When are you coming home?" my father
asked over the phone, as if distance were simply
a matter of miles. This is no gift, this last vigil,
as I watch his hand draw over his face,
his eyes close, as if again he were about to say,
"Well, I guess I've done all I can."

This time there are no words.
Only the brief walk out into the unbelievable
green of May, the buds of Russian olive
already starting to feather, the entire sequence
of a season come to rest in this blossom
that I twist from the branch,

bruise against the swell of my hand
as if its heavy fragrance could revive in me
all the careless gestures of belief:
salt tossed over one shoulder,
a secret oath sealed in blood, the slender
breastbone pulled apart by a wish.

To tear down is the hardest and best
beginning—the curious musk of black
walnuts broken from their hulls, the oily stain
I spent days rubbing into the weathered slats
of a doorframe, my hands thirsty
as the wood and soon the same rich ochre.

So that now as the entry shawls itself
in brilliant leaves, and the mountain beside me
pulls the sun's deep brim down over its eyes,
I am left with these moments that fall
like the heavy gaze of a sunflower,
tooth by ragged tooth, onto the ground.

Even among trees whose evergreen
is a trick of perpetual loss, I am ready to leave
marks on the shoulders of this past,
become the fulcrum I've seen lovers make
while all around them summer
shouts the last of its children home.

Museum at the Tomb of the Unknowns

I. Ruins

One last, crazy Latin breath,
then all of Pompeii's remaining citizenry,
dogs, too, are caught in the act. And who wouldn't
be petrified, given the slow lava of years
that suddenly rains down on us
with the certainty of Tuesday, that middle child
of Norse descent, our bodies preserved
like the imprint of a trilobite, ribcage,
the hollow crib of our last breath
taken in amazement
when almost without notice,
the world turns molten,
consumes us, then reveals
us, two thousand years later,
fetal and asleep.

II. Archives

Or shoveling bread into ovens,
or looking at the sky
as if to gauge the weather,
as if this could go on day after day,
newscast after newscast, a mother
whose failing sight compels her
to pull her grown son to a halt
by the roadside and point to a graveyard
in the distance. *See? See there?* she tells him.
Those are the rooftops of my village.
Or the letter from Gustav Mohr: *The Masai*
have reported. . . that many times. . .
they have seen lions on Finch-Hatton's grave,
and Dinesen's calm reply,
I must remember to tell him.

III. Mausoleum

Precious little, yet enough, clouds
like swept flour on a slate blue floor,
leaves, their reflection in the pond,
small pillows for those
who can make their bed in water
easily as breathing, which we cannot,
having traded for headboards
farther beyond, blankets of fresh earth
rising like cake, then falling

along the pillars, this edifice pushing us
beyond endurance, beyond despair,
until at last we can bear the weight
of someone else's body on our own—
pine flooring weathered to gray, an earthen
pitcher with its potential of flowers,
even a woodcut over our heads, cream white
and pewter blue, that, from one angle,
could be boughs of cedar heaped with snow,

and from another, the vast flap
of laundry, shirts filled with embrace.
Gone now, what we had called belonging,
those furnishings in the appliquéd dark,
sculpted roses in the carpet,
the accordion fold of a lampshade
that, if called upon, might tell us *this was your life*,
this candle, this adz, these jars
washed to mellow blue, part of a landscape
we thought would never change.

Analogous

Raccoons can be landscapes, reared up on their hind legs
against the fence, body in cat burglar stance, ready for any

tricks the motion sensor attempts. Wrecked cars can be
landscapes—Christmas presents crumpled and torn

in the back seat. Who bought them? And for whom?
Where were they headed before taking this detour?

Who designed the wrapping paper to mimic falling
snow, candy canes? Mirrors can most certainly

be landscapes, reflect whatever comes before them, then
tuck whatever's left down deep in memory's silver pocket.

Wishes can become landscapes, once they are pulled
from the bone, all tinsel and prediction, whistle and grit,

entrusted with fixing on the horizon whatever appears
to be broken or undone. Turkey vultures, though,

are quintessential landscapes. They perch like tilted
weathervanes along the roof line, sample the wind

for that cadaverous scent that lifts these raptors by their
six-foot wingspans to soar on updrafts until they locate

what today's buffet special will be. Then they land
like staggering sailors, hunker down, and begin to eat.

Biblical Terms

In no place am I mentioned, being the last
of parents whose memories toward the end
stubbornly returned to the garden.

Then I was left to cover their nakedness,
to shave my father each morning
though his milk-blue eyes couldn't discern me
from daylight. My mother, too, harnessed against
the guttural rocking of trees, fretted the coarse weave
of her hair—hummed—as every night I prayed
for some entity to relieve this dilemma. Instead,
the sun rose, birds sang out the summer,
nothing appeared, save the persistence

to bathe them daily, rub slow blood
back into their shoulders, rub as I have
been told they rubbed me, unbreathing, blue
as the winter night of my birth. My mother
would tell of how everyone stopped breathing
until they heard the choked gasp, the broken cry—
first mine, then my father's, how he took
me to the stable, slit open a new lamb,
laid me inside the still-warm body.

We buried them today, remembering
that first death, our father's expression
as he slowly opened the earth, how our mother
cradled the body, wouldn't let it go.
None of us knew what it meant.
Tonight, my brother drew water from the creek,
and I let him bathe me.

Family Dynamics

Christ hangs from the curtain rod,
gazing out the window.
His knees pancake the clear glass
because Mary has closed the shutters
on him again. She hates
sunrise, and she gets impatient
with the smudges he makes with his nose
as he watches the robins.

Someday she'll find a wall for him,
or so she says. It's not likely.
She's not one to sacrifice
good wall space, and she wishes
he'd get a job.

Joseph has promised
to hang him out in the workshop
where maybe he'll take up the hammer,
a few nails, make something
of himself.

Joseph never loses faith.
He loves this crazy bastard
like a son.

The Lazarus Method

It's quite an embarrassment,
his lanky frame dragging around
behind you like an ill-seamed quilt,

his skin, the clinging remnants
of a parade that trails him
all the way from the sepulcher

as if someday he might want to
follow it back. Fat chance.
For three days he's been dogging you

like some method worse than death,
saying, "Can't you at least do something
about the *smell*? After all,

I didn't ask for this."
And you want to say
you didn't ask for this, either.

That you were surprised
it worked at all, what with the women
howling in your ear and the lepers

outside clamoring to be cleansed.
You want to say it was all a mistake,
this display at his expense,

that you're sorry, and you want to
make it up to him. But you can tell
his price is far beyond atonement,

as his flesh-ragged fingers
pick at your robes. "You'll pay for this,"
he says. "And I'll be there to see it."

And suddenly you realize why
you've come to love this man, this failing
cadaver who has promised to follow you

all the way to Golgotha if he has to.

A Proper Raising

"Jesus Christ, were you born in a barn?" she would yell,
and then remember that he was, even that first night, incapable
of closing the door behind him. Wherever he went, he left
things open: gaping jaws of wooden drawers spilling socks,

clean T-shirts, underwear. More than once, Joseph yelled
"Son of a bitch!" after splitting his head on a cupboard left ajar.
Worst of all, the front door, letting in flies in the summer,
letting out warmth in the winter. "Do we have to heat

the whole outdoors?" Her voice would rise as she reached
for the knob. "Honestly, do you think we're made out of money?"
Over the years, she did her best to accept all those strangers.
"Leave it open, Ma," he'd say. "We could use some fresh air

in here." How could she deny him, knowing what he did
for a living, though some days she wished for heavy curtains
and a good deadbolt. But this morning, after months of rattling
swords, after the loose tongue and the tight crown of thorns,

after the casting of lots and the spear slipped into the sheath
of his ribs, the shroud swaddling him once more like a newborn,
she gave thanks for the curtain torn asunder, the open tomb,
stone rolled aside to reveal her boy telling the God's honest truth.

II. Stocking Up for the End of Days

The Era of Reduced Expectations

Begin with the onionskin pulse of the eyelids,
the stunted toenails, yellow as old newsprint,
and, impossibly, every conscious memory
of birdsong and jasmine bloom, F-chord

and car exhaust, seizure and glacier-blue sky,
mistake and impromptu dances that transform
the days into flesh, the blood-red moon into meaning.
Then begin to subtract those faithful companions:

the heartbeat, the breath, the familiar curve
of one body tucked into another, the infinite miles
the world travels around itself for no apparent
reason. Yes, go ahead and subtract all of that.

What Must Be Done

First lesson: Goodbye. Wave to loved ones,
goodbye, goodbye. Pretend their shoulders mimic
the crest of a hill, their upraised hand, a spade.

Second lesson: love someone. Live for them.
Believe them when they say they will never
leave you. Ignore the evidence.

Third lesson: let them go. Do not smile.
Take what is yours and close the door.
Do not speak. Do not smile. Do not go back.

Fourth lesson: repeat what you have learned.
Teach others to wave, goodbye, goodbye.
Point them to the door. Teach them to leave.

West Union Cemetery
—For Brandi

"Everybody goes there," she says.
"It's the safest place to learn."
So we drive there after dinner,
the sun coming down through the trees,
the whole world turning like a dog
before the hearth.

At first I try to tell her how to start,
how to synchronize the gas with the clutch,
but the car lurches anyway, and we're off,
crawling among banks of the dead
until at last we pick up speed, glide
like a wagon past rows of weathered

mailboxes: McCallister, Reed, Franklin,
Giroux. I want to read them off to her
as we make the turn, head for the long stretch
of second gear, but I can tell she's more
concerned with shifting than with
the delicate engravings in granite.

Yet there is so much left to tell her,
I think, about momentum, about the grip
of the tires on slick pavement,
about the hazards of driving at night,
about freeways, crosswalks, detours, deadends,
about yielding.

The cemetery closes at eight. There's time,
she says, for one more round before dark,
so we turn down the steep hill between Richfield
and Pike, marble shoulders shrugging off
the grinding gears as far back as Schaefer
and Lutz, as far ahead as our names can travel.

Love Song to My Younger Self

"Where has your beloved gone,
O most beautiful among women?"
—*Song of Solomon 6:1*

To seed, my love, to the dogs
who flank me at the kitchen table
and in the car, heads out the window,

ears fluttering in the air like kite tails
as fence posts tick by, as bullet-pocked
road signs caution me to "Keep Right"

and "Pass with Care," the sweetest advice
of the highway. Where has my beloved gone?
That flaxen-haired girl? That willowy slip?

That self-possessed rider whose mount cleared
every brush-fence, then vanished into the lanky,
gilded aspens? Night falls, as the odometer

rolls over to all zeros, as the dashboard
clock builds time out of little green sticks.
Rumble strips, reflectors, and runaway

truck ramps all remind me to keep my eyes
on the highway, as expansion joints match
the downbeat of Springsteen's "Thunder Road":

Show a little faith, there's magic in the night.
You ain't a beauty, but, hey, you're alright.
And that's alright with me.

A Summer Wind, a Cotton Dress

> "A glance held long and a stolen kiss,
> This is how I remember you best."
> —Richard Shindell, *Blue Divide*

Little fires light themselves in the hearth, like tongues
     of flame that reclaim the Holy Spirit, like pitchforks,

in this clapboard house where mayflies swarm and crackle
     against the porch light. On down, a gas station, a five-and-dime,

and your house, which I can see from the kitchen, where
     clothes on the line billow and collapse, billow and collapse.

For now, this small town holds everything I will ever know
     and have to leave behind: bidden and forbidden glances,

voices from the second-floor landing that warn, *Go no further.*
     Night will fall and you will fall with it. Which is what I want,

for the universe to take up where I leave off, this longing
     so deep, it can hold entire planets in its bottomless pocket,

yet shrink to the size of a finger at the hollow of your neck,
     heart drawing blood from the branch-work of your breathing.

Catch and Release

"I think I fished my way right out of my marriage."
—Overheard on the banks of the Madison River

Not the glitz of fluorescent lure and sinker, but
the elegance of fine hair around a tiny hook, supple cane
or graphite capable of flexing and re-flexing line in sinuous

furls across fast-moving water, just the right choice
of mayfly or caddis, time of day, angle of light
and, really, any fish would bite, though some

can be wary, lightning fast. They strike
and spit before the hook has a chance to set,
prize catch just a glint, a glimpse, ripple of slick

muscle, jewel with every facet shining in the green
beneath, incarnation of everything that must be given
a reason to bite and enough line to be caught.

Who wouldn't be seduced by this landscape,
by persistent changes in the current, chance
of a catch every second or tenth or thirteenth

cast, permission to let go without guilt or remorse?
So unlike the novice who ignores the play in that
same old line, who longs for the one that got away.

Life Lines
—For Bob

Yours runs deep through the palm like a peach cleft
while mine chains itself, widow's thinning braid,

down through side channels, branches, wishbones,
to the wrist's blue-veined delta, never quite visible,

never easy to read. Yet these hands come together:
yours grip-thick, deliberate, while mine land and flap

like startled sparrows, knot-knuckled, yet deft enough
to grasp the moment, hold on like a tick to the flesh.

Like that day on the Madison, when you stomped
the anchor release, and we watched the rope slither

between your wading boots, disappear out the back
of the drift boat. Stunned, ham-fisted, thunder-struck,

you yelled, "Well, goddamn! There goes the anchor!"
with such emphasis that it sounded like a punch line,

while my hands flew up in that dark, undulating
Munch-canvas-of-a-gesture, as we sat petrified

on swivel seats, as the water began to carry us toward
gravel bars, strainers, riffles, rocks, and sweeper trees

that gave way to the hunkering piers of Lyons Bridge.
That's when you shipped the oars with one lunge,

vaulted starboard into the swift waters, while my fingers
taloned themselves to the edge of the shallow boat

sweeping along in the current, leaving you, hip deep,
peering into water, then slogging through river grass

floating like Ophelia's undone hair. That's where you
found the braided rope, streaming around your ankles

like some clever snake looped through the anchor.
You kicked it up, fashioned a dripping lasso, tossed it

across boiling rocks to the boat, where I caught it, metaphor
for what we do every day, this thin line, this holding on.

Stories We Tell Ourselves

She took him as one would take a deep breath
or a second chance, though some days she doubted
her own judgment, as when his silence held them
hostage at the dinner table or rode with them
like a soldier sent to notify the next of kin.

She wondered then if she could ever know him
beyond the familiar stirrup of his collarbone, moles
forming a perfect Cassiopeia on his back, fingers
tying intricate knots in monofilament line. And what
could he possibly know of her? Dust, a whirling skirt

between the windmill and the barn? Scent of juniper,
wild onion beside the garden shed? Her mother's curls
pinned tightly against her scalp, or her father's glacier blue
eyes gone milky with forgetting? How could these mean
anything to anyone but her, divorced as they were

from the lazy swing of the pendulum? And what
of those other lives smoldering now under dry grass?
The stars are still there, she tells herself, *even in daylight.*
Even at night, the sun continues to circle and burn
in a world of space and time. We all should be so lucky.

Robert Falcon Scott's Widow, State Dinner, 1916

"You must be tickled to death by the news
about your husband."
                    —A dinner guest, mistaking
                    Kathleen Scott for Emily Shackleton

Every tongue in London clucks "Shackleton," supplanting
the dead at Verdun, the Dublin uprising, zeppelins, incendiaries,
mustard gas—another failed British hero revered, as some nitwit
dignitary congratulates me on the return of my husband.

I reach for my napkin, pitched like a tent on the bone china,
as Asquith instinctively raises his glass, "To the brave
Polar explorers!" He omits the specifics: the Norwegian flag,
the horsemeat, the 80-knot winds, scurvy, and, of course,

the bodies, eight months preserved "in the heart of the Barrier
snow." I made Cherry-Garrard describe them all: Bowers,
at rest like a babe in bunting, frost branching like wisteria
over the roof of the tent, Wilson, arms crossed, "a blue look

of hope" in his eyes, and my Con, the last to die, burning
what paraffin was left to write "I wasn't a very good husband,
but I hope I shall be a good memory…. Make the boy
interested in natural history if you can…" before struggling

out of his winter gear in the incongruous heat
of freezing. I imagine the glacier's slow crawl
to the sea and lift my glass: to Peary, to Amundsen,
to Shackleton, and to the rest of us, surviving the worst.

Kathleen Scott: Masks for Facial Disfigurement, WWI

I. The Tin Noses Shop

> "Men without noses are very beautiful,
> like antique marbles.
> > —Kathleen Scott to Sir Harold Gillies, Plastic Surgeon

Tonks, himself a surgeon, sketched delicate pastels
to chart Gillies' progress, expressions fixed as a clock,
except where tendons floated beneath a cheekbone,

where a nose had been torn away by shrapnel,
skin and cartilage grafted from the forehead.
It became my calling, wounds so raw only artifice

could bind them: leather harness, plaster casts, painted
masks exquisite as anything I ever sculpted: eggshell thin,
yet durable as Rodin's massive statue, embryonic body bent

on the brink of thinking, each feature buttressed against gravity.
I knew not to flinch. Surgeons and sculptors share similar traits:
a keen eye, a steady hand, sharp tools, the nerve to use them.

II. Captain Taggart and the Scotts Visit the Insect House

> "He wanted to make love to her, so she took him
> to the zoo with Peter instead to see the insect house."
> > —From *A Great Task of Happiness:*
> > *The Life of Kathleen Scott*

Chestnut hair swept into a pompadour, hands and mind
so much like a man's that my desire unnerved me more
than her fingers mapping the knotted scars, plaster cloth

wound tight as a gas mask, then clay to model eye socket,
nose, scorched chin. So naturally I fell in love, endured
the exhibit where we murmured over millipedes, leaf

cutters, tapped the glass to rouse tarantulas, dormant
as hand grenades, as Peter raced from bristletail to dung
beetle to thrip before the Latin names of moths

caught his attention: "Ach-er-on-tia at-ro-pos,"
he sounded out. His mother sketched the emblem
between the wings, added musculature, tendons,

layers of skin. I watched Crumley's head, cracked
like a walnut, come to rest beside me on the sandbag,
all sweetmeats and smoking flesh, before the boy

began to tug at my coat sleeve, "May I see? May I see?"
I lifted him chest-high. "Do you see it, Peter?" He nodded.
"A skull. Like poison. Or pirates. Or like yours, Captain

Taggart, which my mother believes is lovely," while
Kathleen read: "The death's head hawkmoth. From *Acheron*,
river of death, and *Atropos*, the Fate who cuts the thread."

Kathleen Scott Young's Tribute to George Mallory

—For Andy Politz

"This is going to be more like war than mountaineering.
I don't expect to come back."
                    —George Mallory to Geoffrey Keynes after his visit
                        with Robert Falcon Scott's widow, Kathleen, 1924

This is how I would have sculpted you,
face down in a greathouse of granite, dimpled skin
bleached to Carerra white by spindrift scouring
the North Face, gloved fingers anchored in talus

that scatters like pine chips into the Rongbuk abyss,
stick-thin foot resting atop your skewed boot,
as if you believed you might survive, find purchase
in the frozen debris to reclaim your beloved Sandy

on the ledge above, and then, in the embrace of a fine
Burberry weave, follow Odell's disembodied voice
down the North Ridge to Camp VI, on to base camp,

family, commendation, and fame. Instead, the mountain
preserved you as no monument of mine ever could, Everest
holding fast to its own, *quo in loco quem posuit.**

* "In the place where he has set" from Psalm 83:7, read at Mallory's and
Irvine's memorial at St. Paul's Cathedral, London, 1924.

At Death's Door

Little by little, faith and hope give way
      like the moorings of a boat, leaving

only grace, soothing hand that spreads
      across the lap of a field, rises and falls

as if the moon had taken the ocean
      by the corners and flapped it

over the shore like a clean sheet.
      Only metaphor holds: that tiny-cathedral-

lock of a window, the skeleton key's
      pointed finger, the mat that reads

Welcome, the threshold creaking
      under the weight of so many crossing.

Ghost Bikes of the Crescent City

"I crave a place for my grief to land."
—Rudri Patel

They appear to have rooted beside the picket fence,
or the lamppost, or the highway sign closest to impact,
Ground Zero, as it were, just a few feet away. Deprived
of a place to lay their burden down, mourners make

of these installations a vehicle for their grief, an object
lesson for those who brake for squirrels, but blast by
stop signs as if human beings were agile enough
to dodge or outrun a drunk driver, which this cyclist

clearly wasn't, hitting first the windshield, then the curb
with a force that rattled the brain in its cranial bowl
and bent the 10-speed into a kinetic wind sculpture
that backed up Canal Street traffic for hours,

the rear tire still spinning as the ambulance pulled up.
Some ghost bikes are built sturdy—wire baskets, chain
guards, bells clamped to handlebars—the kind families rent
on vacation. But others take on the shape of the impact,

melt like a Dali watch over the lip of the sidewalk. At the corner
of Elysian Fields and St. Claude, a tangled white tower of bikes
lends to airy nothing a local habitation and a name, reminds us
that all things continue to mark the dead with their presence.

Zero to Sixty

I thought my sister might live long enough for one last trip
to the thrift store, one last ride in her low-slung, '65 Mustang
with the radio tuned to the Oldies channel, one last stop
at the streetlight where a pock-faced teen in his father's red

Camaro grins and guns the engine until the light turns green,
and my 80-year-old sister shuts him down—0-to-60
in 7.5 seconds, snapping my head back in a classic car
with no headrest. But no. The cancer was too far advanced.

And her children, old themselves, worked to get her affairs in order
while the aides and I stripped the bed, ran the bath, mopped the floor.
My body took the abuse of being alive in a dying house. Until it didn't.
She was being held hostage, she said. She wanted us all arrested.

When I tried the Ativan, the Haldol, she slapped them away,
telling me I was "really weird," which I couldn't deny. Who else
would rent a car in a pandemic and drive for 10 hours because
their oldest brother had died a few days before, and she didn't

want to face it alone? In two days, she no longer knew me at all,
but her dog still did, so I clipped the leash to her collar, and we walked
down Holmes Drive like this was just any other day, and that crying
and walking a bewildered boxer around the block was perfectly normal.

Making Love During a Terrorist Attack

Auden was only half right: we must love one another
and die, which could explain why the move

to disrobe and lie, belly to belly—even while the world
collapses around us and the bodies of so many,

like pearls, are instantly crushed to dust—suddenly
becomes imperative. After all, we have never been
ones to assume grief can be so easily disentangled

from love, that the ragged cry of desire couldn't
just as well be mistaken for the graveside keen.

Still, better to believe our bodies can't be broken
by the weight of certain loss, that the slant of light
we catch so casually from the corner of our eye

can't possibly carry the method of our death.
Which is why on this exquisite September afternoon,

as the sky erases every contrail, and dust settles
on the faces of those sent to recover what we fear
is lost forever, we hold on to what we can.

Rattlesnake Trail

"The local news reports that runners with earbuds on nature
trails in Texas are being bitten in record numbers."
            —*AP* News Report, June 18, 2018

O desperate rattle when escape is cut off.
O puncturable sneakers and spandex.

O hose-shaped vertebrate intertwined in a den
by the rock garden or bifurcating the asphalt path

warmed to perfection, but shared with bi-peds
and bi-pedalers alike. O markings that blend

with mulch or rotted leaves and thus convey
their presence with the racket of a shaman's

gourd—a button for each season the skin has been shed
in blindness. O cranky tracker of prey, who retreats

if given the chance, but who strikes if cornered, then spills
like cold spaghetti into the underbrush, go your

indigenous way before bystanders and stricken alike
revive enough to shout out, *O my God, did you see that?*

Stocking Up for the End of Days

Where I live, death is a given, easy to mistake
for a stick until it coils and strikes lightning fast
from the blackberry bush on up the food chain:
ground, then berry, then bird, then snake,

and so on. Birds that stay baffle their feathers
to keep warm, little down-filled vests with twig feet.
They swell on the branch, rumpled commuters
who have slept badly on the train and forgotten

their hats. We feed them suet and Nyjer thistle,
white millet and black-oil sunflower seeds.
Creating heat burns energy at four below, so they
rattle the feeders, then sail over to the bare redbud

branches to ruffle it up and wait. We accept
them as family this quarantine season, distant
relatives who come for the holidays and stay
way past their welcome, decimating the eggnog,

then singing every cumulative Christmas song
ever written. I try to act like I know what I'm doing,
but what on earth does a person stock up on
that covers both Christmas and the End of Days?

Empty shelves alert me that Clorox, toilet paper,
rice, beans, and beer must top one list, but what
about candy canes, fudge made with marshmallow
creme, sugar cookies, pumpkin pie, those disgusting

Swiss Colony fruitcakes that no one ever eats? God knows,
they would keep. I give up on preparing for the worst.
Let the survivalists stockpile provisions. Let them open fire.
Let them try to keep things the way they never were.

The Lost Child Poem

"There is no word for a parent who loses a child.
That's how awful the loss is."
—Jay Neugeboren, *An Orphan's Tale*

Since that day, I have carried your weight with me.
Since the gurney and curtain with ball bearing casters.
Since the countdown on the lunar-module screen

that was supposed to stay at one number, Icelandic
mountains that were supposed to repeat, not hiccup
or stutter or simply flatten out like a roadmap.

Not this scenario, the one with electrodes, cannula,
orbital-sander paddles smeared with conductive jelly,
ready to jump you into to a place and time,

this place and time, with me as your only advocate.
How wrong is this, baby girl, barely a guest at your own
party, barely there at all, then buried deep in apologies?

I carry your weight with me the way mothers
are born with all the eggs they will ever produce,
as far back as DNA's Möbius braid can be traced,

for as long as the blood cord has tied mother to child
so one can flow into the next and the next and the next,
every life we have ever lost, still with us, in the flesh.

The Heaven of Lost Limbs

Like pets, the amputated are said to have no place,
but here it is, like the hold under a false-bottomed boat,

one gray-green eyeball, plucked by the tail of Lucifer
after the fall, assigned to this severed annex, watching
each extremity as it scuttles toward atonement.

On the left, the amphitheater collects and pairs hands
for shaking or clapping. On the right, legs gather to follow

feet-and-arrow patterns for waltz, tango, merengue,
and Foxtrot, while the more athletic peel off for the stadium
beyond, galloping like renegades from a sack race.

As for feet alone, they try on every style of steel-toed shoe,
or pair off on the beach to make symmetrical prints, a dimly

remembered pursuit before frostbite, land mine, diabetes
and farm accident took a toll. And what of the smaller losses?
Sociable fingers count themselves to ten, or intertwine,

while others, uneasy being alone, adorn themselves
with rings, or tie strings to themselves out of habit.

Toes reunite to wiggle. More rare, the ears affixed
like snails to the wall or the ground, or noses wedged
into whatever they damn well please. And finally

one solitary tongue, neither civil nor tied, gives voice
to all phantom limbs, sings the severed world whole.

Human Nature

It's almost vaudeville how this man
could be any of us out cutting wood
on a sub-zero morning when,

as Frost wrote, *the blade bit flesh,*
and like that, his hand drops
like a clipped bird in the snow.

Yet unlike most of us, he reaches
for the bandana in his pocket,
and with his mouth and other hand,

cinches it around the ragged
sleeve, tendons, bone glistening
like gristle on a rare steak,

and with the fortitude of one
who sees what needs to be done,
and then does it, drives himself

to the hospital, arrives
in time to discover he has
forgotten the hand.

Which is more like us than anything

for him to say, "Well I'll be go to hell,"
as the nurse hooks up the plasma,
as the orderly goes back

to retrieve it. But of course,
it doesn't end with the hand, by now
perfectly preserved by oversight

and snow, or the orderly who carries it
back in a cooler, or even the surgeon
who successfully reconnects it.

It ends, of course, with us

looking on as if something miraculous
has happened—as if it could happen
to any of us.

The Company Misery Loves
—For June Berkley

Say you came back, as the dead are rumored
to do. What snow would dust the doorstep
of your leaving? What sunrise would welcome

you back? What moon would cast its watery gaze
across the river like a lantern floating lit in the black water?
You, who sat and listened to the lives of the hired hands

who worked your father's fields, poor in every sense
of the word, and the Cantwells, aptly named, whose
asbestos-clad shack up the hollow from your farm

defied the creosote fate of a chimney fire
only to succumb to a deluge that swept the house
down the mountain and buried the family

under mud the thickness and color of cow manure,
even the youngest, who hung on his mother's skirts
like a rag torn from the larger, scratchy fabric

of his father. All at the mercy of weather and neglect,
expected to give and take, but mostly give. And then some.
No wonder you believe that everything should end

when you do, emptied of all the calendar days stacked
like shipping crates, emptied of clocks that wring their hands
over the same backward countdown every day. Somewhere

in this void may be the kind of afterlife you could live with,
or be willing to die for: where you are loved beyond all reason,
without having to earn it, without having to pay.

That Evening Sun

Let me end this song on a not-so-minor note,
rest my head on this Gibson L-1, sing goodbye

to every lyric I have ever learned: the one about the boat
that can carry two and the lonesome picker, the one

about how Louise rode home on the mail train
and how walking is most too slow. And, of course,

the one about riding down the canyon that, even after
forty years, recalls my father on a Saturday night

wrapping the fingers of his left hand with adhesive tape,
swaying and slapping an upright bass in some

small-town dance hall while my mother waltzes
across a floor strewn with corn meal, and my brother

and I fall asleep among coats piled high on folding chairs
against the wall. He once told me music was the one thing

he could rely on, married, as he was, in 1929,
his first child, a girl, born and buried a year later,

a life of lung trouble that finally sent him out West
to either die or get well. At thirty, I took him

at his word, picked up the guitar he gave me
the one around whose neck he wrapped my fingers

and taught me songs that survive on breath alone:
how the water is wide, how I won't be worried long,

how I hate to see that evening sun go down.

Kate Fox's work has appeared in the *Great River Review, New Ohio Review, Green Mountains Review, Kenyon Review, Valparaiso Review, Pleiades,* and *West Branch.* She has also authored two poetry chapbooks: *The Lazarus Method*, chosen for the Wick Poetry Series and published by Kent State University Press, and *Walking Off the Map,* published by Seven Kitchens Press in Cincinnati. She was an Ohio Arts Council Individual Artist's Grant recipient, and her poem, "The Lost Baby Poem" earned second place in *Cutthroat's* Joy Harjo Poetry Award competition. She lives in Athens, Ohio, with poet and scholar Bob DeMott, and their two English setters, mild-mannered Katie, and ill-mannered Patch.

Photo by Mary Hendrix

Sheila-Na-Gig Editions